Wealth=Income-Expenses

Reaching your full potential
in personal finance by budgeting

Valerie Chan
Achieve with Val Series

DEDICATION

I dedicate this book to my two daughters, Kimberley and Emily ♥♥♥.

They have been instrumental in me writing this book.

PREFACE

Who should use Wealth=Income–Expenses?

You do not have to be in business to use **Wealth=Income–Expenses**. This book is mainly aimed at individuals who require assistance with their day to day finances. You can use this book or recommend it to someone who is grappling with their own financial woes. Of course, business people might find the book useful as well.

You will be pleased to learn that you can manage some aspects of your finance without having to be financially qualified!

How to use Wealth=Income–Expenses?

Wealth=Income–Expenses is a practical book based on some real life experiences and how issues were resolved.

First read **Chapter 1: The Thinking Process** so that you get in the right frame of mind.

The other chapters then explain the mechanisms. Choose the most pressing financial issue you have and, once you have improved one aspect of your finances, it will spur you to do more.

Motivations behind Wealth=Income–Expenses

I believe in good karma. By sharing some of my knowledge of how to manage my own personal finances, you do not have to reinvent the wheel. Saving at least one person from getting into financial trouble will have a positive snowballing effect on other people.

Refer to the **Jargon Buster** page for explanations of some of the terms.

Disclaimer

Wealth=Income–Expenses is for guidance only and does not constitute formal financial advice. I cannot accept any liability for any loss that you may suffer.
The latest UK tax rules for 2015/2016 have been used. Please be aware that these may change over time.

At the time of writing, I have not received any compensation from any of the websites or companies referred to. They were some of the ones I used or of which I am aware.

CONTENTS

CHAPTER 1: THE THINKING PROCESS

Recognising the issue

Do you **accept** that you have a problem in managing your finances?

If not, there is no point in reading this book further. You will be wasting your time.

> **If there is no issue, then there is nothing to fix**

If yes, then you have taken the first **gigantic step**.

If you are reading this book, it means you are seeking help on how to manage your finances.

It is imperative that you recognise that there is a problem. It is indicative that you care enough to want to change things.

Recognising a weakness is not a weakness in itself.

> **It takes courage for a person to admit their weaknesses**

Why do you want to improve your finances?

What brings you to this book? Is someone pushing you to manage your finances better? There is a tendency to do the opposite when you are not doing things of your own accord.

WEALTH=INCOME-EXPENSES

At the first hurdle, you are likely to give up as subconsciously you are going to prove to the other person that you cannot manage your financial situation.

> **You must want to effect the change yourself**

It is difficult to get a smoker to stop smoking. Likewise, you cannot force a drug addict to stop taking harmful substances. They must be willing to alter their own lives.

Are you at the end of your tether? If you have done the same thing over and over again, then you will get the same results.

> **You need to make changes**

It takes an even **stronger** person to make the necessary changes. **Modifications** are necessary to give you a **different outcome**. Find the **reasons** why you want to improve your finances. They will push you through the tough times. It is like setting out in a car, not knowing where you are going. As such, you will be unsure of the routes to take.

> **I improved my finances for the sake of my children**

Have a think. What is **driving** you? Have pictures to represent it, such as a picture of your children. During the tough times, having something **tangible** to remind you of your purposes will forge you ahead.

> **Myth: You are not doing financially well because of the bad economy**

If this is the case, why are some people doing extremely well in a bad economy? More food for thought!

Rocky roads/paths

I will be honest with you. It will not all be plain sailing. It will not be easy at first as you will not be used to adjusting the way in which you do things.

If something is going to be hard, I will not coat it in sugar candy. I will let you know so that you can anticipate it. I make no apologies for being realistic or for how things are.

You can take a **break**. But come back with a renewed zest.

Causes

With any problem, you need to know what went wrong. You can then find a solution. If you do not know what the problem is in the first place, you cannot expect to get it resolved.

> **Diagnosis is crucial**

Examine how you got in your current financial situation:
- Maybe, like me, your relationship broke down.

- You (or your partner) may have recently lost your job.

- You may have had to take a pay cut.

- You may never have been taught how to manage your money properly.

- As a result of bad habits, you got into the same pattern of spending.

- Your desire to spend like the Joneses may have landed you in hot water.

> **Take a quiet moment to reflect**

As far as I am concerned, I know where I went wrong. I did not keep my eye on the ball. I was not checking my bills or credit card or bank statements and assumed that all was well.

WEALTH=INCOME-EXPENSES

> **Do not make any assumptions; get the facts**

Treatments
Similar to doctors, you need to ask all kinds of questions to find the causes, and then prescribe appropriate treatments. The severity of the causes will lead to different treatments. Dire financial situations will require drastic changes.

Do
❖ Be honest with yourself.

❖ Use money as a means of achieving your dreams.

❖ Take ownership of your actions or inactions.

Don't
❖ View money as a be all and end all.

❖ Mistakenly think that all your worries will fade away once you are financially better off.

How to keep going
Does the sea (or even Tsunami) of emotions **resonate** with you:
- Feeling trapped
- Having panic attacks
- Feeling deflated
- Feeling desperate?

I have lived with what you are going through.

Acknowledge your emotions. Hold those wretched feelings for a few seconds. Feel the pain. I am not being cruel to you. It is a process that I went through to be able to heal.

Now reflect on the very things that are holding you back.

> **I will do my utmost not to have these negative feelings again**

By you not wanting to have these horrible feelings again, you will find ways to change your financial dilemma.

You can now go **YES!** ☺

> ## Do not give up - whatever happens!

Unexpected events will happen in our lives.

But if you take some of the suggestions, you can get out of your financial crisis. You are not alone. That is why I wanted to write this book. There is light at the end of the tunnel.

Rest assured that other people have gone through what you are experiencing and they have come out of it so they are proof that you can resolve your financial crisis. There are precedences to follow. Some of the legwork has been done for you.

Your focus

What you are thinking will reflect in your actions. Focusing on the lack of money will make it worse. All your energy will be focused on justifying the fact that you do not have enough money. It is like having a magnifying glass.

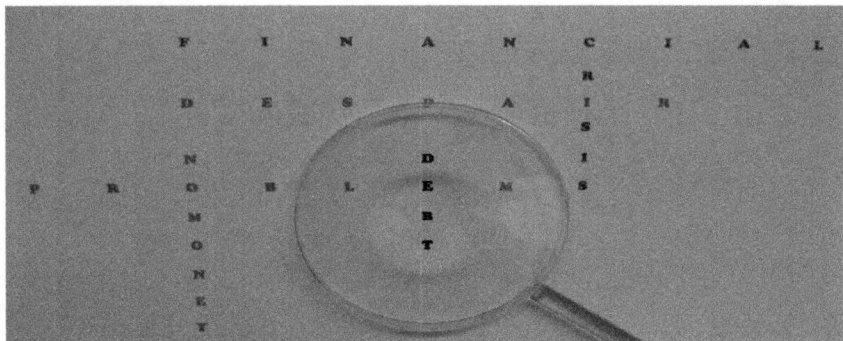

Change your focus to how to spend your money wisely and how you can have alternative income sources. It will be time well spent.

WEALTH=INCOME-EXPENSES

> **Do not panic**

Wealth=Income–Expenses will guide you step by step.

> **Take a deep breath, smile and here we go ….**

Camera, action and roll... **Achieve With Val.**

CHAPTER 2: EXPENSES

Why review your expenses?
The aim of reviewing your expenses is to not live like a miser. **Wealth=Income–Expenses** will enable you to turn around your dire financial situation, and improve your life.

By monitoring how and what you spend, gradually you will have more pounds (that's in terms of money hopefully, not weight around the tummy!)

Do not let money dictate your life. It should be the other way round; you should be able to **control** how you spend your hard earned cash.

> **Get everyone in your household involved. Otherwise one person might be reckless, and it will be a losing battle getting your finances back on track.**

Break down expenses to determine which need to be reduced immediately or which you can do without.

What is the difference between needs and wants?
Compare your **needs** and **wants**.

Needs are what you require for survival.

You should be able to pay for bare necessities such as food, water, shelter and clothing. If not, you are considered to be in absolute poverty.

Wants are things that you would like to have. They are not necessary and you can do without them.

Once you have satisfied your **needs**, extra income can be spent on **wants** such as designer clothes, luxury cars and expensive holidays. Some people spend all their money on their **wants** and then they wonder why they cannot manage their life.
Rein in your expenses until you get back on track. You can use this as your focus.

WEALTH=INCOME-EXPENSES

I have heard some people say:

> ## "I am afraid to open my mail"

Burying your head in the sand can make matters worse. Your situation may not be as bad as you think. It can sometimes be resolved with a few tweaks.

To stop yourself spending mindlessly, think of how many **hours** you will have to work to pay for something. Suppose,

At the end of one month, you earn £1,200.
Excluding weekends, there are 22 working days in a month.
Let's say, you work 7 hours a day.
Your hourly rate will be £1,200 divided by 22 divided by 7 = £7.79.
If you were to buy something for £100, you would have to work
£100 divided by £7.79 = 12.8 hours!
It just put things into perspective.

Don't have the time
I have provided you with a breakdown of expenses in the following chapters, and how to manage each of them. If you do not have the time, implement changes on only one of your biggest expenses. You will be amazed at the **metamorphosis** in your finances!

You will not know until you try some of my suggestions.

CHAPTER 3: EXPENSES - GROCERIES

Groceries include food, drinks and household goods.

> **Do you know exactly how much you spend on groceries in a month?**

You will be surprised how groceries are big spends for most households. It is the biggest expenditure over which you can have control.

Before going out shopping
I make a meal plan of what I will cook during the week. For example:
- Ratatouille, i.e. roast lamb chops with aubergines, peppers and courgettes with lots of rosemary, thyme, basil, salt and pepper.

- Steamed seabass with fried onions, garlic, spring onions and soya sauce. Rougaille i.e. fried onions and garlic with chopped tomatoes and coriander, accompanied by steamed rice.

- Curry with chicken and potatoes, accompanied by poppadums and naan bread. You can add frozen peas in the curry if you like.

- Smoked salmon with mashed potatoes and dwarf beans.

- Mee Foon soup i.e. Chinese rice vermicelli with Chinese mushrooms, pork and cos lettuce.

- Spaghetti meatballs with lots of tomato sauce. I sometimes replace the meatballs with mixed seafood.

- Spare ribs in barbecue sauce, accompanied by asparagus in garlic butter and roasted potatoes. I sometimes replace the spare ribs with roast chicken. Instead of asparagus, I cook white mushrooms and courgettes.

- Steak with lots of onions, chips and a vegetable.

WEALTH=INCOME-EXPENSES

My mouth is watering as I am writing about these dishes. I hope that they inspire you to cook your own meals. Have fun swapping some of the ingredients if you wish.

As you can see, saving money does not mean boring food, or lack of variety. It is how you plan your shopping.

Do
❖ Buy all the necessary ingredients.

❖ As you would already have an idea of what to cook and you have all the ingredients, the cooking can be done in no time.

❖ Check your cupboards, fridge and freezer for what you have so that you do not buy the same things again.

❖ Make a **shopping list** as it will make you realise whether you are overbuying.

❖ It might be cheaper and healthier to cook at home rather than buy take-away, ready meals or processed foods.

❖ I sometimes buy meat on offer such as "3 for £10". I split them into separate bags and freeze them. As and when I need them, I defrost them.

❖ You can buy special offers such as "Buy One Get One Free" on non-perishable essential items such as toothpaste and hand soaps.

❖ Obtain meal or recipe ideas from http://www.nhs.uk/Change4Life/Pages/meal-planner-recipe-finder.aspx.

❖ Have a backup plan, such as if an emergency happens and you cannot cook food from fresh. Once in a while, cook food from your freezer such as pizza, scampi, chips, peas, sweetcorn, etc.

❖ Always check dates when shopping for food, especially those that are perishable.

❖ Bin food after "**use by date**", in particular dairy products, meat and seafood which are not safe to eat.

❖ Discard eggs after "**best before date**" as they may contain salmonella. This is a bacteria that can cause food poisoning, leading to an infection of the gut.

Don't

❖ Grab all the special promotions on offer. You might not actually need them.

❖ Try not to do lots of little shopping almost every day. You are likely to spend more.

❖ By picking up the biggest trolley, you will tend to fill it up and buy more.

❖ Shop when you are hungry. Again, you will tend to buy more.

❖ Necessarily throw away foods after "best before date". They are eatable (except for eggs), but they may not be as fresh as when bought. They may lose some flavours and texture. Such foods are pasta, pulses and cereals.

How to compare cheaper prices
When goods are on promotion, it does not necessarily mean that they are cheaper.

Do

❖ Use the same basis of comparison. For example, compare the prices per 100 grams (these are normally shown on the labels).

❖ Sometimes individual products are cheaper than the promotional packs. Use the calculator on your mobile phone.

WEALTH=INCOME-EXPENSES

Don't

❖ Just look at the one cabinet where there is a mixture of offers. Go to the particular section such as cheeses, and you will be surprised that other products may be cheaper.

Vouchers/clubcard points
Do

❖ Check the voucher expiry date.

❖ Collect your clubcard points when doing your shopping. Some people do not bother but the points do add up into £'s.

Don't

❖ Forget to redeem your clubcard points. I managed to get £50 off my grocery bill when I redeemed my points at one of the leading supermarkets.

❖ Buy only for the sake of collecting points.

Brand names
There are four main brand levels:

1. Premium brands are often in nicer packaging. Sometimes descriptions evoke a feeling of luxury, richness, opulence, sumptuousness and wellbeing.

2. There are also manufacturers' branded products such as Cadbury chocolate or Heinz baked beans.

3. Supermarkets may also have their own brands. You might be astonished that the taste is not as bad and the quality not as inferior as you think.

4. Value brands tend to use words such as "savers".

If it does not tickle your taste buds, then go one brand up. Change brand levels according to what you can afford.

At the checkout
Do

❖ Obtain your refund there and then for any overcharges.

Don't
❖ Just walk away without checking your receipts.

Anecdotes:

At one of the leading supermarkets, I bought a seabass with other groceries. The cashier put through the seabass twice. At another store, the same thing happened when I bought two boxes of spare ribs and I was charged for three!

Prices on the shelves are changed manually but these may not necessarily be reflected on the computer system. Once I bought six litres of water in a pack but I was charged at their individual prices which turned out to be more expensive. On another day, I bought some chicken which was on promotion but the price was not reduced at the till. Human errors occur.

I have been overcharged on more than one occasion at different stores. I reckon other people like you may have also been in the same situation but may be unaware of it!

Food waste = Time wasted
My number one pet hate is food waste. My thinking process of how not to waste food:

1. Think of the time you spent earning money to buy your groceries.

2. Instead of spending your money on wasted food, you could have spent your money elsewhere (opportunity cost).

3. You sometimes trudge to the shops and spend money on transportation.

4. You spend time storing the food away, and then

5. You have to throw the food away!

Do
❖ Check expiry dates before buying goods.

❖ Put your food waste in recycling bins available from some councils.

WEALTH=INCOME-EXPENSES

You will know you have achieved your goals when you have used up almost everything in your fridge or freezer. Only sauces left!

❖ The less time you spend on buying groceries and ending up throwing them away will lead to more **free time** to do what you want and **more money** in your pocket! Thus killing many birds with one stone.

Don't
❖ Let the rotten food spoil your other good food.

At the end of one week, if your fridge/cupboard is still full, it is a clear indication that you are overbuying.

CHAPTER 4: EXPENSES - CREDIT CARDS

Credit score
Credit score is a measure of the risk of poor payment or non-payment based on available data.

> **Myth: Do not have debt!**

You may pay for everything with hard cash, or use your debit card where payments are taken from your bank account within three days or so. Potential lenders do not know if you are a good payer or not as there will be no record of your "credit".

Suppose someone asks you to lend them some money. If that person has borrowed in the past, and he has been bad at paying the money back, you will be on your guard. The risks of lending will be higher. You might give the person a shorter period to repay you, and/or you might charge them higher interest on late payments, and/or you might decide not to lend this person money.

On the other hand, if that person has never borrowed any money from anyone, you have no previous instances to go by.

Credit reference agencies
You can access your credit score by registering with the following credit reference agencies:

- Experian;
- Equifax;
- Callcredit; and
- Noddle [with this one, you can subscribe for **free** for life]

You can use checkmyfile (http://www.checkmyfile.com) to obtain your credit reports from multiple agencies. The first 30 days are free, and you can cancel at any time.

WEALTH=INCOME-EXPENSES

Why do you need to check your credit report?

> **Checking your credit report does not lower your credit score**

1. The acceptance of your application for a loan, mortgage, new bank account or mobile phone contract will depend on your credit score.

2. A good credit rating provides you with access to the best deals with the most competitive interest rate.

3. If your personal details such as your name, date of birth, address and past addresses are incorrect, you might not be identified appropriately.

4. If you do not recognise some accounts opened in your name, it may be that fraud is being committed.

5. The credit reference agencies might have made mistakes on your payment records. You will need to contact them.

6. You might have a County Court Judgement (CCJ), i.e. a court action against you without your knowledge.

7. You need to register to vote at your current address. If you are not on the electoral roll, your credit score is likely to be reduced.

8. When one of my friends was at university, his bank account was overdrawn. He ignored all the bank requests to get his account in order. His debt was sent to a collection agency. This stayed on his credit report for seven years!

9. If there has been a change in your circumstances, this needs to be reflected on your credit report. If your name is financially associated with your ex-partner, you should write to the relevant credit reference agency to have this amended. You should then have a perfect credit score!

VALERIE CHAN

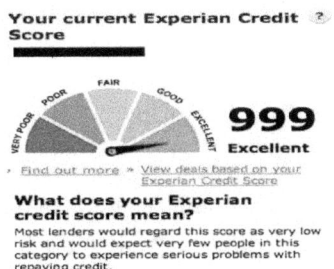

Your current Experian Credit Score

999 Excellent

> Find out more » View deals based on your Experian Credit Score

What does your Experian credit score mean?
Most lenders would regard this score as very low risk and would expect very few people in this category to experience serious problems with repaying credit.

Increases in credit card
Your credit card company may write to you with an increase in their interest rate.

Do
❖ Contact the company within 60 days to reject the rise.

❖ Repay everything you owe at the old rate.

Don't
❖ Spend any more on this credit card.

Consolidating your debts
Do
❖ Consolidate your loans only if they cost you **less than** your current borrowing agreements.

Don't
❖ You may be charged a higher interest rate.

❖ Secure the loan against your home. If you do not keep up with your payments, your home may be repossessed.

❖ Repayments are spread over an unsuitably long period.

0% Credit cards
❖ You can get an **interest free** credit card for up to 23 months.

❖ It means that, during the given period, you will pay a minimum amount every month without being charged interest.

WEALTH=INCOME-EXPENSES

Do

❖ Use the spare money wisely. See the later chapters on income on how to use the extra money.

❖ Set up direct debits so as to not miss any payments.

Don't

❖ Forget to put a reminder for yourself of the end of the interest free period. The interest rate on such a credit card will tend to be high as the credit card providers are well aware that some people will forget to settle their debt.

My debts

I have always been careful with my money. I was a workaholic, and raising my two children was my priority.

During my divorce, I discovered that I was in credit card debt of £59,000 with a bank overdraft! My heart sank. It felt like a big slap in the face.

As part of the divorce settlement, we had to sell some of the other properties that we owned. I cleared my old debts but, even today, I still follow some of the valuable lessons I learnt.

Do

❖ Learn from your mistakes and move forward.

❖ Look at the positives in a bad situation. As a result of my financial troubles, I am more compassionate towards other people, especially my clients in my accountancy business, VF Accountants.

❖ Contact your credit card providers to cancel any second card users to prevent them from spending any more. If you are the main card user, you are liable for any debt.

❖ This debt is too huge for you to deal with it on your own. Your local library may be able to provide you with details of your local Citizens Advice Bureau (CAB).

❖ The Citizens Advice Bureau will require you to prepare a budget. See **Chapter 25: Budget**.

❖ The Citizens Advice Bureau arranged with my credit card providers to stop any further interest charges. Repayment amounts were then agreed.

❖ On an A4 piece of paper, put:

- The credit card name
- Account reference
- Outstanding loan amount and
- Agreed monthly amount to be paid

❖ Cross off each payment that you make. You will gain a sense of accomplishment which will spur you on to reduce your debt.

Don't

❖ Use your credit cards to incur more debt as you will be charged interest at the standard rate!

❖ Succumb to the constant phone calls and letters from your credit card providers chasing you to settle their debt first. I had to go back to the Citizens Advice Bureau and they wrote letters to the credit card providers reminding them of the agreed repayment amounts.

Hot tips on credit card usage

1. If you need to make a big purchase, if possible, delay it until just after your credit card statement date. You may have up to 56 days before you have to pay this money over to your credit card provider. Just remember you still have to pay your credit card on time.

2. Some credit cards offer cashback on your shopping. You spend money on your credit card, then the following month or at the end of the year, your credit card provider will deduct a certain percentage. If you have to spend anyway, you might as well get some money back.

CHAPTER 5: EXPENSES – MORTGAGE

Owning a property is a **need** for shelter. However the size of the property may be dictated by your **wants** such as an extension, a big garden, etc.

Do

❖ Ask friends and family if they can recommend a mortgage broker who can find a better deal for you.

❖ If your mortgage lender charges you more interest than you can earn on your bank account, you would be financially better off paying some of the capital on your mortgage. Check for any early repayment fees.

❖ With time, as you progress through your job, you may earn more income, and be able to afford a better property.

> **"I do not use all the rooms in my property"**

❖ If you do not need all the space, you may be better off selling your current place and finding a smaller one. Alternatively, look at **Chapter 24: Income – How to earn extra income**

Don't

❖ It does not mean that you clear all the money in your bank account, as you need to live and to save in case of an emergency.

❖ Get a mortgage which is beyond your current means.

❖ Assume that, when a property is in joint names, if one person refuses to contribute to the mortgage, your mortgage provider will be sympathetic. They will still send in the bailiffs as it does not matter to them who pays the mortgage as long as it is settled!

> **"You may lose your home if you do not keep up with your mortgage payments"**

CHAPTER 6: EXPENSES – RENT

Renting can be costly. In addition, the property does not belong to you.

Do
- ❖ You need to get contents insurance for your belongings inside the rented property. You could do some research on some of the following websites to find the best deals:
  - http://www.moneysupermarket.com/home-insurance/tenants-insurance/
  - http://www.comparethemarket.com/home-insurance/contents/
  - http://www.confused.com/campaign/home-insurance/tenants-content-insurance/
  - http://www.gocompare.com/tenants-insurance/
  - http://www.directline.com/home-insurance/tenants-contents/
  - http://www.aviva.co.uk/home/contents-cover.html/

- ❖ You may have been a good tenant, keeping the property in good condition and paying your rent on time. An unexpected event may occur causing you to default on your payments. Advise your landlord and ask for an extension on your rent payment. If you don't ask, you don't get.

Just do not abuse the situation and expect to stay rent free for an extended period of time as it is not fair to put the strain on your landlord.

❖ If you are renting an unfurnished or part furnished property, you can get some of your furniture, fridge, TV, etc., for free on https://www.freecycle.org/ or http://www.ilovefreegle.org/

Don't
❖ Go into a property without first inspecting it and completing an inventory.

❖ Sign a tenancy agreement if you do not agree with it as it can be costly trying to get out of a contract.

❖ Pay council tax if you are a student.

CHAPTER 7: EXPENSES – CLOTHING

Do
- ❖ As far as possible, wait for promotional sales to buy clothes.

- ❖ You can even shop out of season. Buy spring and summer clothes in autumn, and buy winter clothes at bargain prices at the start of spring.

- ❖ Search online as you can bag yourself some bargains.

- ❖ Obtain your discount vouchers via websites such as
    - http://www.myvouchercodes.co.uk

    - http://www.discountvouchers.co.uk/

- ❖ You can even get some cashback by registering with these websites:
    - http://www.topcashback.co.uk/

    - http://www.quidco.com/

Date:	4th January 2015
Retailer:	Quidco Compare Follow for retailer
Purchase amount:	£293.81
Cashback amount:	£27.23

Don't
- ❖ It would be a waste of time and money to buy clothes which you will never wear.

- ❖ Forget to use your coupon if you have one. I keep mine in my purse.

CHAPTER 8: EXPENSES - ENTERTAINMENT

Entertainment includes eating out, take-aways, days out and social drinks.

Do
❖ Instead of eating out, buy a few things from the supermarket and make your own.

❖ Plan your meals when there are deals such as "Tuesdays Pizzas Buy One Get One Free".

❖ Eat on a full stomach at home before heading out to the cinema as their popcorn and other snacks can be expensive.

❖ Use discount voucher websites such as :

   - http://www.tastecard.co.uk/

   - http://www.groupon.co.uk/

   - http://www.wowcher.co.uk/deals/national-deal/

   - https://www.livingsocial.com/

Don't
❖ Overindulge on food or drinks. Everything in moderation!

❖ Forget to cancel your direct debit on things such as Sky TV if you no longer watch it.

CHAPTER 9: EXPENSES – UTILITIES

How to reduce your utility bills
Do

❖ Gather all clothes and iron them once a week.

❖ Check your utility bills for accuracy.

❖ Pay by direct debit to get an extra reduction in your utility bills. In addition, you will not forget to pay your gas and electricity on time.

❖ You also pay less if you access your bills online rather than ask for paper copies.

❖ You can greatly reduce your electricity bill by checking the **off peak hours** with your supplier.

❖ Provide **actual readings** for your gas and electricity so that you can compare every year and between suppliers. Read further on how to do this.

❖ If you are **in credit** with your previous utility supplier, do not forget to chase them for a **refund**!

❖ Buy draught proofing strips from DIY shops for your windows and doors.

❖ Change your single glazed windows to double or triple glazing to save on your energy bills. In addition, the home will be warmer and quieter.

❖ Turn down your thermostat by at least 1°C. Wear warmer clothes if you feel cold.

❖ Make use of Apps which let you control the temperature in your home whilst you are away.

❖ Use energy saving light bulbs which also last at least ten times longer than traditional ones.

❖ Draw your curtains at dusk to keep the heat inside the rooms.

❖ If you use a kettle, only put in the amount of water you need.

❖ If your boiler is over 15 years old, you are better off replacing it with a modern boiler system. It can cut your bills by 30-40%. Contact the Energy Saving Advice Service on 0300 123 1234 to see if you can get a grant.

❖ You may be entitled to free loft or cavity wall insulation if you are on certain benefits. Again, contact the Energy Saving Advice Service.

❖ Look for the best deals by going to websites such as:
  - http://www.uswitch.com/gas-electricity/

  - https://switch.which.co.uk/

  - http://www.moneysupermarket.com/gas-and-electricity/

  - http://www.moneysavingexpert.com/cheapenergyclub/

❖ If you find a cheaper deal, mention it to your supplier. They might match the price so as to not lose you as a customer. I changed supplier and I got £100 cashback on my first bill.

❖ When the energy provider quotes you their prices, keep a note of the date, time, prices and to whom you spoke. You will then have relevant information to pursue any complaints. The supplier will know that you are on the ball, and will not try to pull a fast one on you.

❖ **Review** all documents received either by post or by emails. I was changing energy supplier. They quoted me a lower price over the phone than what they had in the new contract. I questioned it, the energy provider listened to the phone call again and I was right.

Don't
❖ Stick to one supplier only as you might be missing out on some substantial savings.

❖ Automatically choose the cheapest company. It has to suit your needs.

❖ Choose a cheap utility company with bad customer service. Google them. They normally cause lots of headaches for their customers.

WEALTH=INCOME-EXPENSES

❖ It is such a waste to leave the light on in a room that is not in use.

❖ Leave equipment such as TVs and computers on standby as they use up energy.

How to extract information from your utility bills

Most people get put off by the amount of information, terminology and figures on their utility bills. Take your latest utility bill and the previous three quarters to give you a whole year's figures.

Your electricity use in detail

Your 0.89p/kWh Direct Debit discount has already been applied to your unit rates.

Meter number

13 Sep 2014 – we read your meter	90475
4 Dec 2014 – we read your meter	90837
Actual kWh used over 83 days	**362.00**

Your gas use in detail

Your 0.3p/kWh Direct Debit discount has already been applied to your unit rates.

Meter number

13 Sep 2014 – we read your meter	6005
4 Dec 2014 – we read your meter	6046
Actual units used over 83 days	41
(Unit calorific value for this period 39.1)	
Gas units converted into kWh	**1288.73**

☞You could create your own table or use the simplified table I have devised.

Quarter	Period	Gas in kWh	Electricity in kWh
1			
2			
3			
4			
	Total usage per year		

It is best not to compare only one quarter of your bill. Your usage is likely to differ depending on whether it is winter, spring, summer or autumn.

CHAPTER 10: EXPENSES – WATER BILLS

Metered charges

Water meters are the fairest way to pay for your water, as you only pay for the amount of water you use, plus a fixed charge.

So you might try this option. If it does not suit your needs, then you might be better off changing back.

With two small children at home, it was difficult to monitor them and prevent them from wasting any water. I had to change from metered charges to unmetered ones. You have to notify your water provider within 12 months of the water meter being fitted, or within one month of your second metered bill.

> **Be aware that the next person who buys your house will be automatically on metered water charges**

Money-saving devices

Even if you do not use a water meter, you can still save money. Ask your water supplier if they provide the following for free:

- A shower head which does not reduce the water pressure but still allows you to use less water.

- Showersave which reduces the use of water and which is screwed at the bottom of your shower hose.

- A shower timer to ensure that you shower within four minutes!

Shower! Shower! Shower!

CHAPTER 11: EXPENSES – COUNCIL TAX

Council tax bands

The councils use the values of properties as at 1991 to determine the amount of council tax you should pay!

Band	Property value in 1991 in England
A	Up to £40,000 and including
B	Over £40,001 and up to £52,000
C	Over £52,001 and up to £68,000
D	Over £68,001 and up to £88,000
E	Over £88,001 and up to £120,000
F	Over £120,001 and up to £160,000
G	Over £160,001 and up to £320,000
H	Over £320,000

Council Band Ranges of Value in England

Do

❖ Search for your council tax band by entering your postcode at Directgov on http://cti.voa.gov.uk/cti/inits.asp. Similar sized properties should have the same council tax bands.

❖ Inform your local council if you no longer live with your partner and/or live with your children. You will be entitled to a single person **discount** of 25% off your council tax bill.

❖ If you have a student living with you, check that your council tax bill does not include the student as they should not pay this.

❖ If your property is unoccupied for a maximum period of six weeks, you may be able to get 100% discount on your council tax.

WEALTH=INCOME-EXPENSES

❖ A property may be uninhabitable due to structural alteration or major repair. For such unoccupied properties, you may get a 25% reduction in your council tax.

❖ If there is someone with disabilities in your household, your council tax bill may be reduced by one band.

❖ You can write to your local council and get them to spread your council tax from the usual 10 months to 12 months! I successfully did mine. It helps in spreading the costs.

Don't

❖ Leave your property unfurnished or unoccupied for more than two years. You can be charged council tax of 150% based on the band in which your property falls.

❖ Fail to pay your council tax as you may be sent to prison for up to three months!

CHAPTER 12: EXPENSES – HOME INSURANCE

Do
- ❖ If you are working from home, advise your home insurance company. Protect visitors to your premises.

- ❖ Save time by having an A4 piece of paper at the front of your expenses folder. Write your home insurance details as they are likely to be the same every year.

- ❖ Use websites to compare prices:

  - http://www.uswitch.com/home-insurance/

  - http://www.gocompare.com/home-insurance/

  - http://www.moneysupermarket.com/home-insurance/

  - http://www.confused.com/home-insurance/

  - http://www.halifax.co.uk/insurance/home-insurance/

- ❖ You can get quotations up to 90 days prior to renewal. You can gain if the cost of home insurance rises in the future as the prices will be locked.

- ❖ Double check what your home insurance covers.

Don't
- ❖ Take out insurances when you are already covered elsewhere. For example, you may be unaware that you have taken out multiple insurance cover for your mobile phones. You can only make one claim in any case.

- ❖ Auto renew your home insurance.

> **A retired couple did not own a computer. They never changed their home insurance provider for over 30 years! I found cheaper home insurance online for them, and they even haggled with a new provider. Their insurance got further reduced, saving them overall some £400!**

CHAPTER 13: EXPENSES – PETROL/DIESEL

Do

❖ Subscribe to www.petrolprices.com to find the cheapest prices near you.

❖ My friends and I take it in turn to drive if we are going to the same destination.

Don't

❖ Forget to earn points at some petrol stations and claim your cashback.

❖ Fill your fuel tank to the maximum as you will be adding too much weight to the car and waste fuel.

❖ Carry a roof rack. The engine has to work harder and will use up more fuel.

❖ Accelerate or break abruptly as you waste fuel.

CHAPTER 14: EXPENSES – MOTOR INSURANCE

Do

❖ Add a second responsible driver such as one of your parents as this may reduce your car insurance significantly.

❖ Did you know that the riskier your job, the higher your premium? So choose the **best job description**. But do not lie.

❖ Research cheaper car insurance by going to some of these websites:
  - http://www.gocompare.com/car-insurance/

  - http://www.moneysupermarket.com/car-insurance/

  - https://www.comparethemarket.com/car-insurance/ (You may get 2 for 1 cinema tickets or claim a meerkat toy!)

  - http://www.aviva.co.uk/car/

  - http://www.confused.com/car-insurance (You may get a "Brian the Robot" toy.)

  - http://www.uswitch.com/car-insurance/

  - http://www.directline.com/car-insurance/

❖ As far as possible pay for your car insurance outright. You will pay a high rate of interest if you choose to pay monthly.

❖ Reduce your bill by adding security features such as an alarm or immobiliser.

WEALTH=INCOME-EXPENSES

❖ Haggle to get your insurer to beat or match your best quotation.

❖ Check your policy carefully for any mistakes.

❖ If you cannot afford to buy a car, you can hire one using Zipcar (http://www.zipcar.co.uk). An IT consultant told me that it was not worth him buying a car. As most of his clients are within a few miles of each other, he takes advantage of the 60 free miles per day! No need to worry about car insurance as it is included in the price.

Don't

❖ Auto renew your car insurance as you may save with another provider.

❖ Necessarily choose third party cover. Insurers view this as more risky and will price higher.

❖ Automatically buy add-ons such as windscreen cover or breakdown. Research for those separately as they may turn out to be cheaper.

❖ The more you modify your car such as adding fancy wheels, the more the insurers will charge you.

CHAPTER 15: EXPENSES – TELEPHONE

Do

❖ Go for paper-free billing. You will be emailed when your bill is ready to view.

❖ Pay your telephone bills by direct debit. It will be one less worry for you in respect of missing payments.

❖ Be aware that most free calls only last up to one hour. Put the phone down after one hour and redial.

❖ Subscribe to Skype for free phone calls, including international calls. You can even use a webcam.

Don't

❖ As far as possible, make phone calls during peak hours as the calls are more expensive. Most phone providers' peak hours are between 7.00am and 7.00pm.

❖ Just switch phone provider as they may beat or match your best deal.

CHAPTER 16: EXPENSES – MOBILE PHONE

Do
- ❖ I use the website http://www.billmonitor.com/ to analyse my mobile phone bills and advise me of better deals. It works for Vodafone, Three and O2.

- ❖ Use the following websites to compare mobile phones deals:
  - http://www.carphonewarehouse.com/mobiles/compare/

  - http://www.confused.com/mobile-phones/

  - http://www.moneysupermarket.com/mobile-phones/latest-mobile-phones/

  - http://www.uswitch.com/mobiles/

- ❖ If you are a heavy user and want to spread your cost, then a contract with a handset will suit you.

- ❖ Whereas if you already have a handset and just want flexibility, then a sim-only contract may be more appropriate.

- ❖ Make the most of the features on your mobile phone. For example, if you have an Iphone, you could use Facetime which is free, provided that there are internet connections.

- ❖ If you do not have an Iphone, subscribe for free to http://www.viber.com/en/products/android. Provided that the other person is also on Viber, you both get free calls and texts. You need internet connections, and you must have an android phone.

- ❖ Whenever possible, use free wi-fi to keep your data costs down.

- ❖ Ensure that your data roaming is off when going on holiday otherwise you will be hit with huge bills.

Don't
- ❖ Opt for a new handset if your current one is in good order as you will be paying for it through a higher tariff.

CHAPTER 17: EXPENSES - MISCELLANEOUS

Timing of purchases

Did you know that, if you timed your purchases in the right month, you can save yourself a **bargain**? Most products are discounted as follows:

MONTH	PRODUCTS
January	Electronics such as printers, fax machines, DVD players and satnavs
February	Kitchen appliances such as washing machines, dishwashers and fridge freezers
March	Cars of older models
April	DIY such as paint
May	Cameras which are end of line
June	Older models TVs
July	4x4s
August	Laptops
September	Kettles
October	Garden furniture
November	Convertible and sports cars
December	Coffee machines

Presents

What is the point of giving an expensive present that someone will never use?

I always think of the recipient's interests and hobbies. For example, if the person likes riding a bicycle, give them some accessories. They don't have to be expensive.

Rather than buy something off the shelf, you may even make it. For example, if you are good at baking, you could make some treats and package them nicely. If you are good at carpentry, you could make a simple piece of furniture.

After all, it is the thought that counts. The recipient is more likely to appreciate the time and effort you have put into the present.

When you do not have much to spend, that is when you become more creative. You use whatever resources you have available.

Parking
Look for parking on http://en.parkopedia.co.uk/ and there is also an app. Type in the postcode and it will tell you if parking is free or how much it will cost. It helps me plan ahead when I have to visit clients, family or friends.

Storage
Are you paying for storage? Is it really necessary?

See my tips on how to create additional income by **decluttering** in **Chapter 24: Income = How to earn extra income**.

CHAPTER 18: INCOME

What is Income?
Income is money or other forms of payment received from employment, investments, universal credit, etc.

Do
❖ Having money is **sweet sorrow**. You need to know how to manage it.

❖ You have to be smart on how you use your time and money efficiently.

❖ Find value in what you do, and get people to pay you for it.

❖ You need to have contingencies in place (a back-up plan).

Don't
❖ Think that earning money means that you have to slave away.

❖ Be too reliant on only one source of income such as your salary from your employment. If you get sacked, then you are in trouble.

Let's explore some of the different possible sources of income, and how to increase them in legitimate ways.

CHAPTER 19: INCOME – SAVINGS

Image courtesy of Stuart Miles
at FreeDigitalphotos.net

Do

❖ Make your money work for you rather than the other way round. Imagine, whilst you are sleeping, you are still earning money!

❖ Track down any bank accounts that you might have forgotten about.

❖ As far as possible, you need to have a back-up plan. Start putting aside a small amount of money; it can be as little as £1.00 per day. It is recommended that you put aside enough money to cover at least six months' worth of expenses. How would you then know how much to save if you have no idea what you normally spend? Refer to the previous sections on expenses.

❖ Income tax of 20% is deducted on your bank accounts. However, if your total income is less than £15,600 a year (for 2015/2016), you can **claim tax back** by completing **Form R40** on https://www.gov.uk/government/publications/income-tax-claim-for-repayment-of-tax-deducted-from-savings-and-investments-r40.

❖ Also, if your total income is less than £15,600 a year (for 2015/2016), you can fill in **Form R85** to receive your bank or building society interest without any tax taken off (**gross**). This form can be obtained from your bank or building society.

Don't

❖ Forget to check whether you are earning the best rate of interest on your bank accounts. When was the last time you looked?

George Osborne's summer statement 2015

There has been a major overhaul on savings. From 6 April 2016, if you receive bank interest of £1,000 and you are a basic rate taxpayer (that is, you pay tax at 20%), no income tax will be deducted. For a 40% taxpayer, the first £500 will be tax free.

CHAPTER 20: INCOME – INDIVIDUAL SAVINGS ACCOUNT (ISA)

What is an ISA?
It is a way of saving money in a bank account. There are two types of ISA:
- Cash ISA; or
- Stocks and shares ISA.

Advantages of having an ISA
1. From 6 April 2015, you can save up to £15,240 in an ISA.

2. You do not pay tax on interest you receive.

3. If you put money in an ISA that invests in stocks and shares, you avoid paying Capital Gains Tax (CGT) on any profits you make on sale.

4. No tax is payable on money withdrawn.

5. From 6 April 2015, a spouse will be able to inherit his/her spouse's ISA on death by continuing to benefit from tax-free returns.

New - Help to Buy ISA
The Chancellor announced in his Budget 2015 that, for every £200 per month saved towards a first time buyer's home in a Help to Buy ISA, the Government will give a bonus of £50. The bonus is limited to a maximum of £3,000 per person.

The bonus is available for the purchase of UK properties only. It is available on home purchases of up to £450,000 in London and up to £250,000 outside of London.

CHAPTER 21: INCOME – EMPLOYMENT

Money you receive from your employment is basically calculated as follows:

	£
Gross salary	x
Less: Pension deductions	(x)

Taxable income	x
Less: Income tax	(x)
Less: Employee's National Insurance	(x)

Net salary (take home pay)	x
	===

By understanding the components that make up your salary, you would hopefully understand how your salary can be influenced.

Tax code
Have a look at your tax code on your payslip. For 2015/2016, if you have no other income, then your tax code should be 1060L, meaning that you do not pay any tax on income of up to £10,600. If your circumstances change, you should inform Her Majesty's Revenue and Customs (HMRC).

An acquaintance used to have two jobs but then he dropped one of them. His tax code on his payslip did not reflect that change. His gut feeling that he was paying too much tax was correct. I helped him to get a tax refund of approximately £1,100.

CHAPTER 22: INCOME – PENSION

What is a Pension?
A pension is a way of saving money so that you have an income when you stop working. The UK Government is well aware that people are living longer. Besides, working age people are not making adequate savings for their retirement.

What is Auto-Enrolment?
Do not be scared of some of the words.

In a bid to get workers to save into a pension, Pension Auto Enrolment has been introduced. Employers are required to offer their employees an **option** to save money into a pension scheme.

Do

❖ Weigh up whether you can live on less money in your pocket now, compared with having money to live on in the future.

❖ Read your pension documents carefully. If something is not clear, check with your employer or pension provider.

❖ If a spouse dies before age 75, the other spouse can take the retirement income from an annuity due to them tax-free. An annuity is a guaranteed income each year for the rest of your life.

❖ Seek the advice of an independent financial adviser (IFA).

Don't

❖ Deal with cold callers offering free pension reviews. They may have glossy brochures and fancy websites. They will even promise you high returns but these are unrealistic.

Tax relief on personal pension
How do you obtain tax relief on your personal pension, that is, how do you **save tax**?

VALERIE CHAN

The following example is based on the 2015/2016 tax rules.

As a basic rate taxpayer, you pay tax at 20%. If you contribute £80 towards a pension, the Government will contribute £20. You will then have £100 in a pension pot.

If you are a higher rate taxpayer (that is, you pay tax at 40%), if you contribute £80 towards a pension, the Government will contribute £20. You will also have £100 in a pension pot. However, you can claim back tax of 20%, that is, £20 by completing your **self assessment tax return**. This is subject to an annual allowance of £40,000 for 2015/2016, and you must have paid enough tax. In effect, you would have only paid £60 into your pension.

If you do not pay any income tax, you can put £5,000 for 2015/2016 into a pension plan. You will get tax relief of 20%, that is, a saving of £1,250 resulting in a pension pot of £6,250.

George Osborne, The Chancellor of the Exchequer, also delivered a pension revolution in his 2015 Budget. From 6 April 2015, people aged over 55 can withdraw 25% of their pension savings without any tax implications. Use these lump sums wisely.

CHAPTER 23: INCOME – UNIVERSAL CREDIT

Universal credit is a combination of the following benefits:
- Jobseeker's allowance
- Housing benefit
- Working tax credit
- Child tax credit
- Employment and support allowance
- Income support

As at 2015, the above benefits are paid separately. The universal credit is **one** monthly payment for low income earners or people out of work. Do not fail to claim your benefits if you are entitled. Go onto HMRC website https://www.gov.uk/tax-credits-calculator for further details.

Universal credit will be spread to other parts of the UK. The new system has been introduced in these areas:
- Greater Manchester
- Hammersmith and Fulham
- Bath
- Harrogate
- Rugby and
- Flintshire in Wales

Housing benefits
The Government wants people on housing benefits to take on more responsibilities, and to **learn to manage their finances**. I believe that, without proper training or support, this will prove to be disastrous.

In addition, those councils who have implemented the universal credit have suffered lots of computer glitches.

Instead of paying directly to the landlords, the Government pays rent money to the council tenants. The latter is then expected to pass on the rent to their landlords. In areas where the universal credit has already been implemented, there have been many instances where the council tenants have spent the rent money. This is having an adverse effect on their landlords. Most council tenants do not want the hassle of having to manage their own finances and prefer the old system.

CHAPTER 24: INCOME – HOW TO EARN EXTRA INCOME

I can hear you say:

> **"I am not good at anything"**

Sit down and think of some of the happy or difficult situations you have come across. This will give you an idea of:
- your personality traits such as being an introvert who is good at listening; and
- skills that you could use such as leadership skills to motivate, inspire and build respect.

I have given you plenty of ways to reduce your bills.

> **Money breeds money**

You cannot be completely risk averse; you will never move on in your life. For example, you might think you cannot go out in case you are run down by a car. You will be limiting yourself too much. How about learning how to cross the road safely? So you learn how to **minimise** your risks.

Research the risks involved as much as possible. Weigh up the advantages and disadvantages.

For example, if you are thinking of setting up your own business, talk to as many people as possible who have done so. You will have better ideas of what is involved.

You can turn your hobbies or passions into another source of income. Do not overlook any opportunities. You need to take actions.

Think of problems that you can solve, and earn money from it.

If you are good at making jokes, you could do stand-up comedy.

If you are good at baking cakes, you could use your home kitchen to make birthday or other party cakes.

WEALTH=INCOME-EXPENSES

If you have got rhythm, consider teaching Zumba classes… whatever takes your fancy!

Rent received from your own residence
If you have a spare room in your **own home**, why not let it out? Based on current tax rules for 2015/2016, you do not pay extra tax if you earn up to £4,250 a year. This is known as **Rent a Room Scheme**.

From 6 April 2016, the rent a room limit will be increased to £7,500 following the Summer 2015 budget!

Buy-to-let property
If you own another property and you rent it out, you may have to complete a self assessment (personal) tax return. For the tax year 2015/2016, if your gross income from property exceeds £10,000, you will need to inform Her Majesty's Revenue and Customs (HMRC).

Rent your parking space
You may have an unused driveway, garage or parking space. You could advertise on sites such as Parklet, YourParkingSpace, etc.

Declutter
We often search high and low for things that we do not have. We tend to forget to look at what we already have.

Look at what you have and, if it is not being used, how you can make money out of it.

I am of the opinion that, if you have not used something for more than a year, you are unlikely to need it.

> **You will literally be letting go of baggage!**

Clearing out can also have a **cathartic** effect on your finances. It will be evident what you have and do not have.

Do

❖ Clear your loft, garage, basement and other parts of your property. It will make it look bigger, even your bank account.

❖ Sell on Ebay, Gumtree or at car boot sales.

❖ If you cannot sell, you can give donations to charity. You will feel tremendously satisfied that you have given to a good cause or to other people who need them the most.

❖ Decluttering has positive psychological effects. You will feel lighter and free.

Don't

❖ Rent unnecessary additional storage space.

Hobby vs trading – income tax implications

The occasional sales (such as selling to friends and family) can be the results of your hobby. If you do not set out to make a profit, you will not be considered to be trading.

If you are selling personal items which you have owned for some time, then you are unlikely to be considered to be running a business. You will not have to declare the money you receive in this case.

Once you start selling your goods or services with a view to making profits, you will need to inform Her Majesty's Revenue & Customs (HMRC) within three months. You will need to complete a personal (self assessment) tax return and to keep records of all your transactions.

If you buy things to sell them in auctions, you are most likely to be trading.

Hobby vs trading – capital gains tax (CGT) implications

If you sell, for example, a rental property for more than its original value, you will have to pay CGT if the difference between your sale price and the original value exceeds £11,100. This is based on the UK tax rules for 2015/2016.

If you sell tangible, moveable goods like furniture, paintings, antiques, motor cars, lorries, motorcycles, etc., they are known as chattels. You will have to pay CGT if the difference between your sale price and the original value exceeds £6,000 (based on 2015/2016 tax rules).

WEALTH=INCOME-EXPENSES

These will have to be declared on your personal (self assessment) tax return.

Sell your gadgets
You can sell your unused mobile phone handset on:
- http://www.mazumamobile.com/

- http://www.fonebank.com/

- http://www.envirofone.com/en-gb/envirofone/

- http://www.sellyourhandset.co.uk/

CHAPTER 25: BUDGET

What is a budget?
This word gets used a lot. It can be a scary word for many.

> **A budget is simply what you can afford**

The difference between your income and expenses is what money you are left with.

> **Wealth=Income–Expenses**

Why do you need a budget?
It is better to know your actual financial situation in black and white rather than guess.

You might have money coming in, and think that you are rich. You hear so many stories of Millionaire Lottery winners whose lives went disastrously wrong. They lacked control and management of their money.

Budget layout
This is an example of a budget layout by month.
☞ You can adapt the table according to the type of income and expenses you have.

WEALTH=INCOME-EXPENSES

DESCRIPTION	MONTH
INCOME (MONEY COMING IN)	
Salary	
Bank interest received	
Dividends received	
Tax credits, etc	
Other income	
Total Income	
EXPENSES (WHAT YOU SPEND ON)	
GROCERIES	
Food and household products	
HOME	
Mortgage/rent	
Home insurance	
Home repairs and maintenance such as painting	
Home improvements such as house extension	
Council tax	
UTILITIES	
Gas	
Electricity	
Water	

MOTOR EXPENSES	
Petrol/diesel	
Motor insurance	
Car repairs and maintenance such as MOT	
TRAVELLING EXPENSES	
Bus, rail and tube fares	
Taxis	
TELECOMMUNICATIONS	
Telephone	
Mobile phone	
Internet	
ENTERTAINMENT	
Eating out/takeaways/social drinks	
Hobbies	
Holidays	
MISCELLANEOUS	
Clothing	
Presents	
Grooming (makeup, hair, etc)	
Total Expenses	
Total Income Less Total Expenses	

CHAPTER 26: NEW BEGINNINGS

You should not lead your life just for the sake of earning money. It is what you do with your money that is important; use it as a means to an end. Money should be what you need to enable you to achieve your goals in life, and be happy.

Rest assured in the knowledge that lots of people who have been in similar financial situations have managed to break free. So can you.

You have been given plenty of suggestions on how to reduce your expenses, increase your income and thereby increase your wealth. Savings do add up. It will be time well spent in finding a resolution to your money issues.

There are many aspects of your finances which you can **control** and influence. It will make you feel **empowered**.

I hope that you enjoyed this book, and have or will implement most of the suggestions. Wishing you all the best for all the exciting times ahead.

To new beginnings…**Achieve with Val.**

Please leave your likes and your comments on:

Facebook: http://www.facebook.com/AchieveWithVal

Twitter: http://twitter.com/AchieveWithVal

Website: http://www.achievewithval.com

JARGON BUSTER

Annuity – Guaranteed income each year for the rest of your life.

Auto-enrolment - Employers are required to offer their employees an option to save money into a pension scheme.

Budget – It is an estimate of your expected income and expenses, i.e. what you can afford.

Capital gains tax – Tax that you pay if you sell an item for more than its original value.

Child benefit – It is a payment made to any person who has legal responsibility for a child.

Child tax credit – It is a benefit paid to people who are on a low income who are responsible for at least one child.

Credit score - A measure of the risk of poor payment or non-payment based on available data.

Data roaming - Your phone receives data over mobile networks which your mobile operator does not own.

Dire – Requires urgent attention.

Dividends – Payment made by a company for your shares.

Financial freedom – It is the ability to be who you really are and do what you want in life.

Income - Money or other forms of payment received from employment, investments, etc.

WEALTH=INCOME-EXPENSES

Individual Savings Account (ISA) – A way of saving money in a bank account.

Inflation – A rise in the general price of goods and services.

Karma – Action or deed.

Miser – A person who lives poorly to save money.

Needs - Things that are necessary for your survival.

Opportunity cost – A benefit you have to give up in order to achieve something else.

Pension - A way of saving money so that you have an income when you stop working.

Rent a Room Scheme - You can earn a certain amount a year through letting out furnished accommodation in your home without having to pay any extra tax.

Self assessment tax return – A form on which you declare your income.

Shares – Ownership of a part of a company.

Tax relief – How to save tax.

Universal tax credit – It is a single payment for people who are looking for work or are on a low income.

Uswitch – A comparison website.

Wants – Things that you would like to have. They are not necessary and you can do without them.

Working tax credit – It is a benefit paid to people who work but who are on a low wage. It is an incentive to get people working.

AUTHOR BIOGRAPHY

Valerie Chan juggles household bills, her own business and the lives of her two daughters. She is a divorce survivor, and overcomes adversity through Salsa dancing. One, Two, Three … Five, Six, Seven. Oops had a little salsa moment there!

Valerie was born in Mauritius. Studying Accounting for her GCSE, she discovered her first love. Her passion brought her to the UK to study ACCA (Association of Chartered Certified Accountants). She eventually set up her own accountancy business, VF Accountants.

Through her writing and experiences, Valerie wants to provide you with hope, even if the situation seems dire. With the right tools and support, you can pull through. So go ahead…Achieve With Val.